The
HIGH LAKELAND FELLS

Tom Lawton

© Tom Lawton 1994

Designed by Ian Allan Studio

Published by Dial Press

an imprint of Ian Allan Ltd, Terminal House, Station Approach, Shepperton, Surrey TW17 8AS; and printed by Ian Allan Printing Ltd, Coombelands House, Coombelands Lane, Addlestone, Weybridge, Surrey KT15 1HY.

Left:
Looking down on Derwent Water and Newlands, pointing towards the high Centre Fells.

Back cover:
The north-easterly vista observed from the summit of Wetherlam

Front cover:
Great Langdale valley and Lingmoor Fell viewed from above The Band.

DIAL PRESS

Introduction

The fascinating landscapes of the English Lake District are a unique fusion of tranquil, blue waters; lush, green, wooded valleys; steep-sided, bracken-laden, forested slopes and craggy, purple, rocky mountain peaks. The mountains of this region are called fells, and the highest of these soar to heights above 3,000ft, towering over, and both dominating and protecting, the surrounding countryside. Finger-like fissures and intervening rocky spurs spread out in all directions from the summits of these mighty fells, linking these majestic heights with the flat, glaciated valley floors many hundreds of feet below. In so doing they present countless scenes of sheer perfection. The bands of rock soaring to the dizzy heights above provide safe routes for walkers of most abilities to reach the summits of the high fells along acceptable gradients, and without the need for climbing skills necessary to scale the many more demanding rock faces also abundantly present in these mountains so splendidly shaped by the extreme actions of fire and ice!

Many visitors to Lakeland who gaze in wonder and admiration at these high fells for the first time are likely to experience a compelling urge to walk or scramble up them. Some will make a start on this delightful outdoor leisure activity there and then, impatient to get to the top of one of the summits which particularly catches their admiration. Others will plan their first walking exploration amongst these mountains in a more sober and reflective manner, undertaking this on some future, dedicated occasion — like first thing tomorrow morning!

Most of those who set out for the top will make it without undue difficulty and in doing so will be rewarded with delights that have to be experienced for themselves, not described in books! Some walkers will be more than content to get only part way up, their objectives reflecting their known, more limited, physical capabilities. However, once bitten, both these groups of intrepid walkers are likely to return many times to this enthralling landscape to rekindle on each of these occasions the challenge, contentment and complete fulfilment they find in trekking these high fells, either enveloped in solitude or agreeably sharing these unforgettable experiences with their chosen walking companions.

This book presents a picture story of these high fells, one which is not intended to be merely a passive presentation, but rather a spur to activate you into putting your boots on as an essential preliminary to placing your feet on some, if not all, of the highest points of the many fells captured in these photographs. The very highest of these is Scafell Pike rising to a height of 3,210ft (978m). It also happens to be the highest elevation in the whole of England.

Below this lofty jumble of shattered rocks what other fells should be included in an accurate and comprehensive catalogue of *The High Fells of Lakeland*; and then how should these be conveniently grouped? Any selection and subsequent arrangement will be partly arbitrary and will inevitably reflect both personal preferences and prejudices. The fells chosen for the purposes of this photographic presentation are broadly those commanding a height above 2,500ft. This constraining line is not, however, sacrosanct and some of the more remote and less well-known mountains above 2,500ft have been excluded, whilst certain extremely popular and accessible fells below this height have been covered. This later group include the easily recognized volcanic plug profiles of the Langdale Pikes, together with the superb, ridge terrain spanning Dale Head, Hindscarth and Robinson, for it would be unthinkable to omit these beloved mountains from any classification of the high fells of Lakeland even though their heights are marginally below the arbitrary chosen 2500 foot marker band. (A listing in descending height sequence of the principal fells covered by the photographs, indicating their allocated grouping, is provided in the appendix.)

These high fells have been grouped into 13 convenient geographical configurations. They commence with the Skiddaw plateau in the northern most part of Lakeland, then track roughly from west to east down through and across the National Park to conclude with the most southerly grouping of the discrete Coniston Fells. These chosen groupings are listed below:-

1 Skiddaw and Blencathra
2 Grasmoor and Grisedale Pike
3 Dale Head, Hindscarth and Robinson
4 High Stile Group
5 Pillar Group
6 The Gables
7 The Scafells
8 Bow Fell and Crinkle Crags
9 The Langdale Pikes
10 Helvellyn Group
11 The Fairfield Group
12 High Street and the Easterly Fells
13 The Coniston Fells

On average, six photographs are presented of each one of these thirteen selected mountain groups. These cover a variety of views, some taken on or from around the various summits of each group of fells, whilst other pictures record the configuration of and inter-relationship of every grouping as observed from more distant vantage points. The collection records these high fells observed throughout all seasons of the year, and a balance has been struck between views including walkers together with their accoutrements, and views capturing the solitude of these remote and lofty places. Altogether the 80 or so views present a comprehensive overall perspective of the high fells of Lakeland, revealing and illustrating how they combine and consolidate to form this unique and breathtaking landscape.

A succinct profile of each grouping introduces each section of photographs. This is arranged under the separate headings of **Location**, **Features**, **Principal peaks**, author's **Favourite walking route** and **Other popular walking routes**. In passing it must be recorded that the author's first choice of walking route is biased by his base camp being located in Great Langdale valley and to the consequent ease or difficulty for him in reaching various starting locations situated in more remote parts of Lakeland. Readers will either already have favourite routes, or will come to establish these from starting locations particularly suitable for themselves.

Take care on your explorations into these high places, go well prepared and properly equipped with maps, a reliable compass and appropriate provisions including nourishing food, drink and a first aid pack. Always wear or carry adequate warm and waterproof protective clothing including comfortable boots; also have your camera at the ready! You will then be able to appreciate to the full, with absolute minimum risk, the thrill of standing on the highest parts of this magnificent, mountainous masterpiece glowing in the warmth and satisfaction of your achievements. With a reliable camera only requiring activating, these precious moments may be permanently secured on film.

The metamorphosed slates of Skiddaw are amongst the oldest exposed rocks laid down anywhere in the world; some 600 million years went into their present day shaping, but this time-consuming evolution process which spanned the extremes of volcanic activity and the ravages of successive Ice Ages is fully justified by the captivating landscapes here today for us all to enjoy. George Bernard Shaw is credited with having said, 'Use your health even to the point of wearing it out!' Do not go quite as far as this in scaling the highest fells of Lakeland, but good luck and enjoy yourself to the full in accomplishing any exploration in these mountains, particularly those that you may have been moved to explore by browsing through this picture book.

4

THE HIGH FELLS OF LAKELAND — Selected Groupings

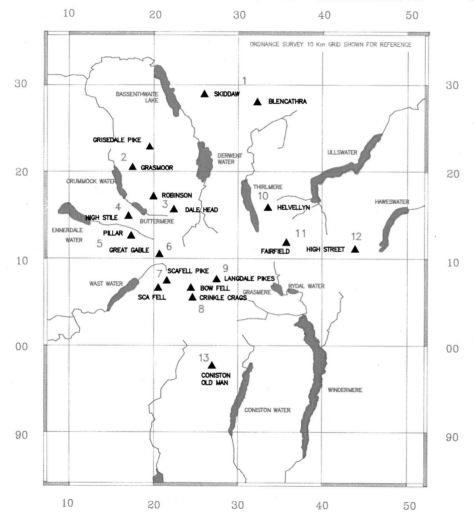

1 SKIDDAW and BLENCATHRA

2 GRASMOOR and GRISEDALE PIKE

3 DALE HEAD, HINDSCARTH and ROBINSON

4 HIGH STILE Group

5 PILLAR Group

6 The GABLES

7 The SCAFELLS

8 BOW FELL and CRINKLE CRAGS

9 The LANGDALE PIKES

10 HELVELLYN Group

11 The FAIRFIELD Group

12 HIGH STREET and the Easterly Fells

13 The CONISTON Fells

1 Skiddaw and Blencathra

Location

The northernmost part of Lakeland towering above Keswick and Threlkeld

Features

Massive open rounded fellsides, punctuated by a series of spectacular arêtes with intervening gouged-out combes.

Principal peaks

Skiddaw : 3,053ft (931m)
Blencathra : 2,847ft (868m)
Little Man: 2,837ft (865m)

Favourite walking route

From Threlkeld climb Blencathra by way of Scales Tarn and Sharp Edge. Descend along Hall's Fell Ridge. (Distance about 8 miles involving 3,000ft of ascent: allow 5 to 6 hours.)

Other popular walking routes

From Keswick climb Skiddaw by circular route via Carl Side.

From Threlkeld walk up Blencathra by either Blease Fell or Scales Fell.

Above:
The frosty heather-clad approach slopes to Causey Pike present revealing views over Newlands and the silted-up flat stretch of land separating Bassenthwaite Lake from Derwent Water. The snow-capped summits of Skiddaw and Blencathra provide a compelling background. I had started out from Braithwaite that day in total darkness, my hands and feet numb with cold, but by the time this photograph was taken I was tingling from the warmth of my exertions up the relentlessly steep slopes of Rowling End.

Left:

The rounded slopes of Carl Side on Skiddaw lead the eyes southwards beyond Keswick and Derwent Water towards the high central fells of Lakeland. The distinctive silhouettes of the Langdale Pikes and the Scafell massif can just be discerned on the far-off horizon. August is the best time to be trampling over these slopes when the profusion of purple heathers in bloom is a joy to behold. The quartz rocks of White Stones make a particularly good perch to stop for refreshments and to absorb this luscious spectacle, before tackling the harsher higher ground leading to the summit of Skiddaw.

Above right:

Lying between the peaks of Skiddaw and Blencathra are the extensive rolling fellsides of Skiddaw Forest. The remoteness of this vast area is punctured by the tiny youth hostel of Skiddaw House nestling within the shelter of a protective copse of conifers and visible towards the centre of the photograph. The shot was taken in December from the upper reaches of Blencathra. You could see for miles that day to the snow-capped peaks of some of the mountains of Scotland captured on the distant horizon. Blencathra was bristling with human activity, but later on I shared the solitude of Skiddaw Forest with only a few hardy sheep.

Right:

The extensive summit area of Skiddaw presents a fine unrestricted viewing platform in all directions. This view is eastwards towards and beyond Blencathra. The many pointed separate peaks of this 'saddleback' of a mountain can be clearly identified from the observation position. Situated amongst the intervening lower terrain is the splendid rounded spur of Sale How. However, do not be tempted to use this as a convenient linkage of these two principal mountains as this will traverse one of our most important areas of heather. This is particularly rich in wildlife and is a site designated as of Special Scientific Interest under the protection of English Nature.

Left:
Striding purposefully down the rocky arête of Sharp Edge in fine style. The edge links the vast summit of Blencathra with the lower ground cradling Scales Tarn. The tarn lies to the south of the ridge nestling in a gouged-out basin blocked by glacial moraines. These walkers were out on a fine, hot, still day during the height of summer and were thus able to move fast, lightly clad and in complete safety. It can be a different story in winter when these edges present formidable challenges even to experienced and properly equipped walkers and climbers, as the following photograph illustrates!

Below left:
Looking down on walkers enjoying the thrill of climbing up Hall's Fell Ridge to the summit of Blencathra on a sunny winter's day. This route commences from above the village of Threlkeld and is regarded by many as one of the finest ridge scrambles anywhere in Lakeland. I had got into position to take this view by walking up the easier approach slopes of Blease Fell. I was the only person that day who I observed equipped with crampons and I made good use of them whilst descending along Sharp Edge. I do implore you to have such items with you when faced with extreme conditions amongst the high fells as it is better to be safe rather than sorry!

2 Grasmoor and Grisedale Pike

Location

The northwesterly fells separating Crummock Water and Derwent Water.

Features

Classical long rounded ridges dividing interposed sheltered valleys. Awesome chasms line north face of Grasmoor.

Principal peaks

Crag Hill : 2,749ft (839m)
Grasmoor : 2,791ft (852m)
Grisedale Pike : 2,593ft (791m)

Favourite walking route

From Braithwaite up Causey Pike and over Crag Hill to Grasmoor. Return via Grisedale Pike. (Distance about 11 miles involving 4,200ft of ascent: allow 7 hours.)

Other popular walking routes

Grasmoor by way of Whiteless Pike from Buttermere.

Ridge route from Grisedale Pike to Whiteside.

Above:
The profiles of the long, parallel ridges leading to the peaks of Grasmoor and Grisedale Pike observed from the wintry slopes of Blease Fell on Blencathra. Many other features are captured in this landscape including part of Derwent Water, Newlands valley and the profiles of Robinson, the High Stile group and far-off Pillar. The snow conditions that day were quite superb: soft, dry powdery stuff that seduced you to walk for miles, which I did. Towards the end of a perfect day on the high fells I was fortunate to witness a most captivating red sunset which sometimes occurs towards the wane of a cloudless, still day and is well worth staying out for.

Left:
Looking down from a great height on the silted-up mouth of Rannerdale. The viewing position was along the easterly edge of Grasmoor. The lake is part of Crummock Water and the rocky spur rising steeply on the far left of the picture is the craggy outline of Rannerdale Knotts which juts out into the lake at Hause Point. My climb that day had been an unusual one for me, from the tranquillity of Buttermere. This route by way of Whiteless Pike can be made into a fast up and down if need be and can be accomplished well within half a day if you push it as I had to do.

Below leftt:
A spectacular sighting northwards from the dangerous crumbling edge of Grasmoor above Dove Crags. Beyond the hanging valley the impressive, serrated, rocky ridges of Gasgale Crags dominate the intermediate ground, whilst the lower fells on the far side of Lorton Vale break up the view beyond of the flat plain extending to the coast. There was frost everywhere that day, even on me, as I lingered long making my way contentedly by the edge and gazing down in wonderment through the massive gaps and chasms savagely torn into the rock-strewn fellside by glacial action and compounded by subsequent weathering.

Right:

A colourfully-clad walker admiring the view down Coledale. Grisedale Pike rises majestically to the north and far beyond this and much further east lies the massive shape of Skiddaw Forest with the peaks of Skiddaw and Blencathra predominant. Coledale is a sheltered valley somewhat disfigured by abandoned mine workings and quarry spoils. The most satisfying route eastwards from the spot where this photograph was taken is along the fine ridge of Grisedale Pike. This was an almost automated selection process for my companion and myself. The valley way is not without recompense though, particularly on a sunny day in late autumn or winter when the profuse, faded, orange-coloured bracken is displayed to its best.

Below right:

Taken against the sun from the glistening rocky summit of Grisedale Pike to reveal the approach of another solitary walker captured against the back-cloth of Crag Hill and Grasmoor. The vastness of these massive remote grassy slopes is revealed in this shot. Every time I reach the top of Grisedale Pike I feel a slight twinge of disappointment at the relatively paltry and precariously perched summit cairn. I have vowed to strengthen this, without necessarily enlarging it, on some future occasion and this I will eventually do unless in the meantime you just happen, without any prompting from me, to beat me to it!

Above:
The steep slopes of Red Pike provide many fine views down across Buttermere and Crummock Water to the massive outline of Grasmoor rising to the north beyond these sheltered waters. The ridges observed leading to the summit area provide fine walking routes, none more so than that up Whiteless Pike and along Whiteless Edge. Although I have observed these views on many occasions, they never cease to thrill me. I was once riveted here with two companions illuminated by the soft yellow light of a most fantastic sunset. One of these walkers never carried a camera with him, but even he on that occasion confessed he wished he could have recorded the views.

3 Dale Head, Hindscarth and Robinson

Location

These three fells and their converging access ridges form an arrowhead from Buttermere pointing towards Derwent Water and Keswick.

Features

An elongated E-shaped series of connecting rocky bands. Broad summit areas contrast with concealed steep, sheer, shattered rock faces. Some good scrambling.

Principal peaks

Dale Head : 2,473ft (753m)
Hindscarth : 2,385ft (727m)
Robinson : 2,417ft (737m)

Favourite walking route

From Gutherscale climb Cat Bells and Maiden Moor to reach Dale Head. Then on to Hindscarth and Robinson before returning down Newlands valley. (Distance about 12 miles involving 4,000ft of ascent: allow 7 hours.)

Other popular walking routes

Perhaps the other way round!

Above:
A distant view from the north of the Dale Head, Hindscarth and Robinson configuration revealed towards the top left hand corner of the photograph. The wide panoramic view from White Stones on Skiddaw shows the position of this mountain group relative to the many other peaks which comprise the northwest fells. From the viewpoint selected it looks as though you could race round this elongated E shape of mountains in very little time. However, the complete Dale Head circuit is quite demanding and involves a full day's walking as I have registered on more than one occasion tramping back along either Newlands or over Cat Bells in the fading light of dusk.

Left:

This photograph was taken in May when the gorse was coming into bloom and is across the flatness of the Newlands valley pointing towards the long ridge linking Cat Bells with Dale Head. The lower part of the valley is quite fertile and successfully farmed. To the west beyond the obscuring ridge lies Borrowdale and Derwent Water. I have trekked up and down the stretch of road just visible in the left hand corner of the shot on numerous occasions *en route* from Braithwaite to either the start of Rowling End or as a necessary preliminary to walking from that village to any combination of Dale Head, Hindscarth or Robinson. This is because I have not discovered a more agreeable route, but if you know differently...!

Below left:

The view northwards along the Cat Bells ridge looking towards the rounded slopes of mighty Skiddaw, on this occasion accentuated by slivers of lingering snow. The several small hamlets nestling beneath the protection of these slopes are marked by a series of white rectangles delineating the positions of individual dwellings. We set out in darkness that particular day in mid-December and were appropriately rewarded for this effort before the cock crowed by enjoying one of those explorations into the high fells that lives in one's memory for ever. Later on, looking down into Borrowdale, the low-lying ground appeared to be covered by inches of frost because for several days the rays of the sun had failed to reach and melt the successive carpets laid down by nightly temperatures well below freezing.

Right:
The splendid summit cairn of Dale Head silhouetted between the distant skyline of the Dodds and the enormous western fellsides culminating in Helvellyn. In between, but unfortunately out of view, are the jewels of Borrowdale and Derwent Water. Our route that day was Dale Head, Hindscarth and Robinson in that sequence. We saw nobody else on these fells during the whole of our walk, except when about half way round we encountered two other stalwarts doing the route the other way round. We exchanged the usual pleasantries before they hurried off; hastily explaining, as they departed in a cloud of snow, that they were shift-workers who had to get back as quickly as possible so as not to be late for their scheduled clocking-on time early that evening.

Below right:
The flat area around the summit of Robinson provides particularly fine views to the south into the central fells. This one across its attractive, partly snow-covered, gentle slopes picks out Bow Fell, Esk Pike, the Scafells, the Gables, and Kirk Fell. I have a particular affection for Robinson because shortly after this photograph was taken I observed in the gathering, swirling mist, and for only the second time in my life, the thrill of the Brocken Spectre. On this occasion there was also present the concentric rainbow-like rings which formed a refracted 'glory' round my shadow. Unfortunately, the constraints of my camera prevented me from satisfactorily recording this momentous mountain phenomenon.

Above:
A view across the rich pastures and wooded areas near Little Town of the steep slopes of Hindscarth and Robinson rising majestically to the southwest. The access roads in this vicinity are extremely narrow and the approach to the point where this photograph was taken is best completed on foot. It was near here, by Newlands Church, that I took my only photograph ever in the great outdoors of an artist's coloured sketch. This was with that person's kind permission and is reproduced in miniature here so that you can have a go at making out who this fine artist is. I will give you an obscure clue: his subject is Grange-in-Borrowdale!

4 High Stile Group

Location

Mountains flanking the south west shoreline of Buttermere and dividing this valley from Ennerdale to the south.

Features

Three contrasting fells joined together by high-level rocky bands. Lower slopes are thickly deciduous wooded or coniferous forested.

Principal peaks

High Crag : 2,443ft (744m)
High Stile : 2,644ft (806m)
Red Pike : 2,479ft (755m)

Favourite walking route

From Buttermere village climb Hay Stacks before dropping down to Scarth Gap as a prelude to walking the ridge in the order High Crag, High Stile and Red Pike. Descend via Scale Force. (Distance about 11 miles involving 3,400ft of ascent: allow 7 hours.)

Other popular walking routes

Climb Red Pike direct from Buttermere by way of The Saddle. Return by either Scale Force or by one of the longer routes over High Stile, High Crag and perhaps Hay Stacks.

Above:
Shot in soft early morning sunlight from near the road leading down to Buttermere village from Newlands Pass. Beyond Buttermere the fine profiles of High Stile and Red Pike dominate the skyline separated by the massive combe which contains Bleaberry Tarn. The scar cut down the fellside by the falling waters of Sourmilk Gill can be clearly discerned. Buttermere holds many fond memories for me and also some less fond ones. Most of the latter occurred many years ago during several very wet camping escapades but fortunately these trials become mellowed by the passing years. However, I can still recall vividly to this day drinking beer from a bottle outside the Fish Inn whilst devouring several Mars bars. This feat was performed after a long, hard day spent without refreshments, roaming the high fells including Pillar, having returned to Buttermere in pitch darkness, with no food at the inn and all their glasses already put to good use!

Left:
The perfectly still sheet of water on the surface of Buttermere makes a fine mirror in faithfully reflecting the snow-capped conical peak of Red Pike rising majestically beyond The Saddle. These lake shores are delightfully wooded with a variety of deciduous trees of which oak predominates. The pleasant walk round the lake is a must for families with young children. If yours are anything like mine were, the highlight of this trip will be walking through the longish, narrow tunnel on the north shoreline. This was cut through the rock, it is purported, on the orders of a zealous landowner to keep his employees suitably occupied and fit when work for them was scarce. For those bound for the high fells, this routeing will enable you to get your muscles toned-up for the more strenuous challenges ahead.

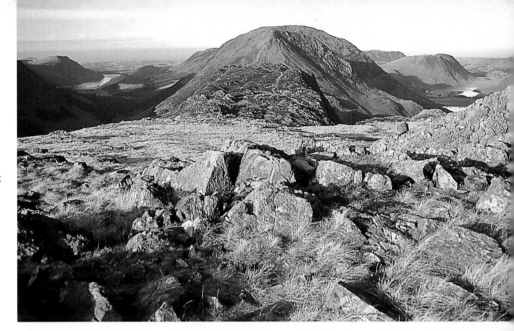

Above right:
The High Stile ridge end-on, taken from the vast slopes around Brandreth. Beyond the craggy profile of Hay Stacks the higher silhouettes of, first, pointed High Crag and then the larger, more rounded slopes of High Stile are visible. The lake to the southwest and on the left is Ennerdale Water, whilst those to the northeast are Buttermere with Crummock Water beyond. Hay Stacks can be a bewildering mystery of paths, tarns, jumbled rocks and scattered summits in wet, misty conditions and walking parties which have included myself have on occasions spent moments up there arguing as to which way to proceed. Fortunately, we have always managed to sort ourselves out in a fairly agreeable manner. However, the northerly faces of this mountain of relatively modest height can be extremely dangerous and over the years there have been unnecessary fatalities. Therefore, do take great care whilst exploring this mountain, particularly in treacherous weather.

Right:
From High Stile and the high-level route from this mountain westwards there are compelling views, such as this one of Red Pike and Bleaberry Tarn comfortably nestling in the combe below. Of all the severely eroded paths littering Lakeland the higher part of the one from Buttermere straight up to the summit of Red Pike — clearly visible on the photograph — is, in my opinion, one of the worst and most dangerous. The word diabolical comes easily to mind in this context. This hazard is well known and extensive permanent renovation work is now being put in hand, or perhaps more correctly, placed under foot.

Left:
The view along the ridge towards High Stile from the summit of Red Pike. Also getting into the picture in the far distance are the tops of the rocky massif that contains Scafell Pike. The best times to be on High Stile or Red Pike are at dawn or at sunset. So far I have never managed it first thing in the morning, but late evening is another matter. At the fading of the sun the views from here, particularly of the northwestern fells, are unbelievably beautiful. On several occasions I have marvelled at the long shadows cast by the setting sun of each mountain ridge on the next one further to the east, the outline of every darker area faithfully following the profile of the particular fells from which it has been cast.

Below left:
During the lower part of the descent from Red Pike towards Buttermere, more detailed views are revealed of the village and of its proximity to the intervening lake of that name. In this view the two usual approach routes to Grasmoor are simultaneously exposed, the longer one from Causey Pike over Crag Hill and the quicker one up Whiteless Pike. The route down to Buttermere from Red Pike can be a little perplexing for first-time users. This is due to the fact that at one point you have to walk away from the direct line down to the village for quite a way before the correct path obligingly traverses back to a more reassuring direction.

Right:
A rare one of the author gazing contentedly down the length of Crummock Water from the slopes of Red Pike before I was rudely told to get out of the way by my walking companion because apparently he also admired this view and wanted to take a decent photograph of it from that very spot!

5 Pillar Group

Location

Horseshoe of mountains cradling Mosedale. Part of the westerly fells separating the upper reaches of Ennerdale from Wasdale.

Features

Rugged, remote high fells offering some superb walking and climbing routes. Severe erosion and rock-shattering with combes, ridges, rock pitches and steep, scree slopes.

Principal peaks

Pillar : 2,927ft (892m) Steeple: 2,687ft (819m) Haycock : 2,618ft (797m) Red Pike Mosedale : 2,707ft (826m)

Favourite walking route

From Buttermere over Scarth Gap and up Black Sail Pass to Pillar. Descend into Ennerdale and then back over Red Pike.(Distance about 13$^{1}/_{2}$ miles involving 5,400ft of ascent: allow a good 9 hours.)

Other popular walking routes

Mosedale Horseshoe route from Wasdale Head climbing Pillar, Steeple, Red Pike and Yewbarrow.

From Borrowdale via Black Sail Pass to Pillar. Descend into Mosedale and return via Sty Head.

Above:

Wasdale Head and the fine grouping of high peaks including Pillar which comprise the Mosedale Horseshoe. The shot was taken from the approach ridge to Scafell Pike from Great End which provides many superb views overlooking Wasdale and the massive mountains to the northwest. The weather on the mid-October day this shot was taken was perfect for photography. From first dawning light to setting sun all I had to do when a view caught my eye, as many did, was to operate the shutter. This without any frustrating wait, whilst becoming frozen in the process, for the sun to appear from behind veiling clouds.

Above:

Just before the sharp right off Gillercomb Head to access the steeper slopes leading to Green Gable, there are a number of small trapped tarns that provide a splendid foreground for the views westwards towards Pillar. These are some of them. These shallow tarns are quite often frozen over and this can occur almost any time save during the height of summer. In these conditions the solid surface makes an almost irresistible target at which to propel small stones in order to test its strength.

Left:

Looking down into upper Ennerdale from one of the many frightening voids lining the long northern flank of Pillar. This one lies to the northwest of the summit in an area where particular care is called for, especially when the approach ground is slippery from melting snow as in the photograph. I have ventured down most of these exacting chasms, but complete honesty forces me to disclose that in most cases this was no more than the short distance necessary to reach the viewing point that had lured me away from the firm ground at the top and my precarious scramble down was usually less than the odd 50ft or so. Only attempt to repeat these precarious manoeuvres using the utmost care!

Above:

Gaining only marginal protection from a bitterly cold north-westerly wind sweeping across the expansive frozen slopes of Pillar. I was obliged to use a very fast shutter speed for this exposure as my companion was only prepared to remain in this position for milliseconds before we re-activated our heat-generating muscles.

We had set out earlier that day from Buttermere and, apart from the exposed top 500ft or so of the highest peaks we scaled, the weather was very pleasant and that part of the walk through the forests of Ennerdale almost uncomfortably warm. However, I too must admit my exposed lower limbs also felt the cold on the top of Pillar.

Right:

A profile of Pillar rock that emerged for seconds through the boughs of an intervening silver birch tree whilst we were making our way, enveloped in swirling mist, up Ennerdale. Based on my observations, low cloud and mist often linger in upper Ennerdale even on days when many parts of Lakeland are bathed in almost unbroken sunshine. The reward is that when the swirling, suspended droplets of water do disperse, and they sometimes do this with a 'twinkling', the sudden revelation of the high craggy fells encircling this valley is simply breathtaking.

Below right:

The long easterly approach profile of Pillar observed across Ennerdale and the closer, still waters of the trapped tarn situated within the summit area of Hay Stacks. I recall the taking of this photograph well, but unfortunately for the wrong reason. It was about 8pm towards the end of a perfect day and my companion and I were enjoying the solitude of the spot, the splendid views and the absolute silence, each of us contentedly deep in thought. Quite abruptly two of the noisiest walkers I have ever encountered amongst the fells appeared and proceeded to impress each other with a loud and irritating recapitulation of their knowledge of the surrounding terrain. We quickly moved off and consoled ourselves at Innominate Tarn which was equally delightful and far less noisy.

6 The Gables

Location

Dominant mountain grouping standing at the head of and between Wasdale, Ennerdale and the upper reaches of Borrowdale. Allen Crags and Glaramara to the east have been included in this grouping.

Features

Great Gable is a huge dome-shaped jumble of rocks overshadowing the smaller and more rounded slopes of Green Gable. Challenging climbs and scrambles abound.

Principal peaks

Green Gable : 2,628ft (801m)
Great Gable : 2,949ft (899m)
Allen Crags : 2,572ft (785m)
Glaramara : 2,560ft (781m)

Favourite walking route

From Seatoller climb Great Gable by way of Brandreth and Green Gable. Return over Allen Crags and Glaramara (Distance about 11 miles involving 4,500ft of ascent: allow 8 hours.)

Other popular walking routes

From Great Gable very strong walkers could also climb Scafell Pike by means of the Corridor Route.

Scale Great Gable from the top of Honister Pass and return by way of Kirk Fell and possibly also include Hay Stacks.

Above:
The distinctive gable-end profile of Great Gable seen from a less visited viewpoint along Kirk Fell to the west. Some of the many climbing faces lining the slopes of this huge chunk of rock are discernible. Kirk Fell is not the easiest of mountains to reach and it is therefore one which even walkers well experienced in tramping over the high Lakeland fells may still have to become familiar with. You will not be disappointed when you do, and the crossing from Great Gable linking this to the top of Black Sail Pass is a popular and extremely useful walking route.

Right:
Looking down along Wast Water from the jumble of rocks just below the summit of Great Gable happens to be one of my favourite views, as it may also be of other walkers such as the two obliging stalwarts captured in this unposed photograph. Normally the top of Great Gable is for me a 4 minute summit! This is just enough time to hurriedly devour some refreshments whilst enduring a challenging cocktail of freezing temperatures, high winds, chilling, swirling mists and minimum visibility. There are, however, exceptions such as the day this photograph was taken when we lingered contentedly for over an hour sipping our Château Grand Mayne 1984 at a much more agreeable rate.

Above:

The steep slopes of Great Gable are a formidable mixture of rock pitches, shattered boulders, stones and loose scree. These features are admirably exposed in the view from near the summit looking down towards White Napes. You will, however, need to scramble down a short distance from the top to observe this. On the occasion this photograph was taken we chatted for some time to three delightful, mature ladies, who between them had achieved a far wider range of visits to the summit of this mountain than we will ever accomplish. For one it was her first expedition but another had been up there on no less than 80 separate occasions.

Above:

Although Green Gable is situated in the almost permanent shadow of its better-known big brother, it nevertheless is a fine mountain in its own right. This view of it from the higher slopes of Great Gable also includes Dale Head in the middle distance and the far-away profiles of Skiddaw and Blencathra. Green Gable represents for many walkers the final resting spot before their attempt to reach the top of Great Gable. The gentle terrain on its summit is the perfect spot for contemplation and for recharging the batteries amongst the most rewarding views, of which those towards the Scafells are amongst some of the best.

Left:

It was over Easter when this photograph was taken of two walkers approaching Esk Hause from Sty Head. The mountains forming the back-cloth are Great and Green Gables divided by the fault-line of Aaron Slack. At the time I was *en route* from Great Gable to Glaramara. The latter is a much neglected mountain, for reasons I have never been able to fathom. The ridge walk from Allen Crags is great and long, the adventurous descent into Borrowdale is, in my opinion, one of the best in Lakeland.

Above:

The stony and quite expansive western shoulder of Great Gable provides many fine viewing platforms overlooking Kirk Fell. This one captures the bulk of this lower but huge saddle-back of a mountain, and this bulk leads the eye to the captivating circular profile of the Mosedale Horseshoe splendidly displayed beyond. I have yet to discover an ascent or descent of Great Gable which was not demanding, and that towards Kirk Fell is no exception. It is fortunate that we all believe the rewards for doing this time and time again are always well worth the effort.

7 The Scafells

Location

The central, massive, mountainous pivot of Lakeland, lying to the east of Wasdale, the west of the Langdales, the south of Borrowdale and the north of Eskdale.

Features

The highest elevation in England. Composed of barren, rock-shattered, eroded slopes of tangled boulders and precipitous voids. Quite magnificent wild mountainous scenery radiates in all directions.

Principal peaks

Scafell Pike : 3,210ft (978m)
Sca Fell : 3,162ft (964m)
Broad Crag : 3,100ft (945m)
Ill Crag : 3,070ft (935m)
Great End : 2,984ft (910m)

Favourite walking route

Mickleden, and via Rossett Gill to Scafell Pike. Return over Esk Pike and Bow Fell.(Distance about 12 miles involving 4,200ft of ascent: allow 8 hours.)

Other popular walking routes

Climb Scafell Pike from Wasdale taking in Lingmell Crag.

Starting from Wrynose Bottom there is an extremely strenuous route over Bow Fell, Scafell Pike and Sca Fell.

Above:
Occasionally the Scafell Group is covered in a mantle of white to portray a winter wonderland. This was one such rare occasion and the view is from the slopes leading to Dow Crag in the Coniston Fells. The distant peaks include Sca Fell, Scafell Pike, Ill and Broad Crags, Great End, Esk Pike and Bow Fell. Snow, snow everywhere and not a drop to spare was the order of the day. Fortunately my walking companions on that occasion were so keen to go everywhere and to see everything that they only had time to hurl the odd snowball in my direction and then their aim was not particularly accurate.

Right:
From the depths of winter to the heat of approaching summer. Towards Wasdale Head is a popular starting point for directly scaling the Scafells as it presents some of the swiftest approach routes. This view of these two walkers setting out with the peaks immediately ahead beckoning them serves to illustrate this. Wasdale Head can be all things to all men and women. It is not the easiest place to get to either self or mechanically propelled. However, it is a spot to be cherished; remote, wild, hospitable, at times hopelessly overcrowded but always a welcome refuge and a super launching pad for expeditions into the surrounding high fells.

Left:
Great End and the awesome bulk of Scafell Pike appearing above wispy clouds during a descent from Great Gable. The far off peaks towards the left of the photograph are Esk Pike and Bow Fell. The point from which this photograph was taken and the summit of Scafell Pike are linked by a challenging walk described as the Corridor Route. I have only ever trekked this way once and that was in the company of a group of comedians who walked from Stonethwaite in Borrowdale, over Great Gable, then on to Scafell Pike along the Corridor Route, before condescending to return for tea to the farm we were staying at by way of Glaramara. Perhaps I do understand why I have never ventured along here twice.

Above right:
A view of the rocky easterly slopes of Lingmell captured from near the summit of Scafell Pike. The encircling mountains forming the background are Pillar and the other peaks, including Red Pike, which form the giant Mosedale Horseshoe. The Mosedale Horseshoe is a really great walk involving some testing scrambling of which, in my opinion, the highlight is the extension of scaling the exposed pitches on Stirrup Crag leading to Yewbarrow.

Right:
The craggy outline of Sca Fell observed from the summit area of Scafell Pike. The compelling views westwards from the top of this barren, rocky elevation must rank as some of the best and most impressive to be seen anywhere in Lakeland. On particularly fine days, and these often occur during the period from late autumn to early spring, there is sometimes 'no-room at the inn' on the summit of Scafell Pike. The inn in this context being the dominant, squarish, uppermost cairn which most walkers appear eager to stand on, and why not? On such days the best times to avoid the rush are outside the short interval between the hours of 10am and 4pm, when you will probably even be able to evade accidentally bumping into my group.

The Romans knew what they were doing when they built their forts in such commanding positions. The one I have in mind here is Mediobogdum above Eskdale and as you can see this provides excellent views across upper Eskdale and Lingcove towards the mighty Scafell massif. I have walked round the sturdy walls of this fortress on many occasions contemplating what conditions the soldiers billeted there had to endure both in terms of weather and the harsh military disciplines that no doubt were imposed upon them. In doing this I usually forgot all about the relatively minor discomfort signals generated by my wet feet sustained by walking across the soggy ground between the roadway and the fort in footwear totally inappropriate for this purpose.

Right:
An unusual sighting of Scafell Pike almost obliterated under mountains of snow.

8 Bow Fell and Crinkle Crags

Location

Above the western extremities of Great Langdale valley.

Features

Craggy, boulder-strewn mountains with distinctive helmet-shaped, pointed peaks. Mixture of rocky buttresses and more accessible spurs and bands.

Principal peaks

Bow Fell : 2,960ft (902m)
Esk Pike : 2,903ft (885m)
Crinkle Crags : 2,816ft (859m)

Favourite walking route

Repeat of favourite Scafell Pike route which involves scaling Bow Fell. (See page 32). Another favourite is to climb Pike of Blisco from Great Langdale and then to scramble over Crinkle Crags *en route* to Bow Fell. The return is via Angle Tarn and Rossett Gill.(Distance about 10 miles involving 4,200ft of ascent: allow 7 hours.)

Other popular walking routes

It is possible to access both Crinkle Crags and Bow Fell from south and southwesterly routes commencing from either Wrynose Bottom or Eskdale. However, some of these involve long and strenuous approaches over waterlogged terrain.

Above:
Occupying centre-stage is the snow-capped peak of Bow Fell flanked to the south by Crinkle Crags and to the north by the Langdale Pikes. The view is from the slopes rising to the Fairfield Horseshoe on which far less snow was lying. Walking on Bow Fell, particularly in cloud or mist, requires care. This is because, apart from the usual physical dangers to be avoided in these high places, the rocks of Bow Fell contain minerals with magnetic properties that render compass bearings hereabouts suspect. It is quite easy even for experienced walkers to start to descend into the wrong valley system from this pivotal peak and it is a long way from Eskdale to Great Langdale!

Above:
The infamous Bad Step on Crinkle Crags with walkers displaying a variety of ways of how and how not to get above it. For most of us the correct way is to scale the rock slabs to the right of the fault when approaching this from below. This recommended route affords sound foot and hand holds and with a little stretching most walkers will experience minimum difficulty getting up this obstacle. For those who do not fancy doing this there is an easier route to the west round the step, but if you do decide to take this way be careful to track back to your right towards the top of the gully to re-engage with the main path northwards.

Above:
The magnificent view southwards when descending from the summit area of Bow Fell taking in Three Tarns, Crinkle Crags, the Coniston fells, Red Tarn and Pike of Blisco. On a fine, sunny day try to delay your descent from Bow Fell until as late as possible in order to observe the panoramic views from along here in their 'perfection' format. However, remember it is a long way to almost anywhere from this area and for example the demanding trek down The Band to reach Great Langdale takes quite a time, even when 'motoring' along this in a hurry.

Left:
The proud peak of Bow Fell silhouetted below the faraway horizon of the Pennines. The walker in the foreground is picking his way down the boulder-strewn summit slopes of Scafell Pike. One of my recommended walks takes in both of these high fells and entails a long but immensely enjoyable day immersed amongst these mighty peaks. Sometime towards the height of summer on a fine sunny day of your choosing endeavour to spend longer than usual up here and explore every mound, nook and cranny contained along the rocky band stretching from Great End to Scafell Pike. You will be well rewarded for these efforts and you will observe some quite unexpected views.

Below left:
Below the mighty westerly cradle formed by the precipitous rocky slopes of Esk Pike and Bow Fell there nestles a tiny tarn and a sheep. The waters are Angle Tarn but I cannot immediately recall the name of the inquisitive sheep who was determined to get into my picture. *En route* from Mickleden to Esk Hause after overcoming the rigours of climbing up Rossett Gill a stop beside the tranquil waters of Angle Tarn is almost obligatory. Some walkers who are also skilled in the arts of bathing remain here all day also soaking-in whatever sunshine breaks through. I have been tempted on occasions to do this myself during particularly hot days but, like cats, I usually find myself able to resist allowing myself to become immersed in ice cold water.

Right:
See what I mean about delaying your departure from Bow Fell until the last possible moment. This view taken from near the Three Tarns at about 8pm is looking westwards towards Eskdale. At the time this regressive landscape was illuminated by the most fascinating colours which I might amateurishly describe as a range of Chinese reddish hues. Do try sometime to wander in the vicinity of the Three Tarns in the evening. The sunsets from here can be superb and in addition to those of Eskdale, there is a particularly fine view across the tarns of the gaunt, dark silhouette of the Scafells rearing-up defiantly against the setting sun.

9 The Langdale Pikes

Location

The Langdale Pikes stand sentinel over the northerly flank of Mickleden and the upper reaches of Great Langdale valley.

Features

Craggy, dome-shaped volcanic plugs that provide a riveting horizon from all view points. Excellent scrambling including the much trodden and fingered exposed route to the summit of Pavey Ark by way of Jack's Rake.

Principal peaks

Sergeant Man : 2,414ft (736m)
Pavey Ark : 2,288ft (697m)
Harrison Stickle : 2,403ft (732m)
Pike of Stickle: 2,323ft (708m)

Favourite walking route

Starting from Grasmere walk up Easedale to Sergeant Man. Descend to Stickle Tarn and use Jack's Rake to reach the summit of Pavey Ark. Then cross to Harrison Stickle prior to descending back to Stickle Tarn. Return along Blea Rigg and Silver How. (Distance about 10 miles involving 3,600ft of ascent: allow 7 hours.)

Other popular walking routes

From Grasmere use Silver How and Blea Rigg to reach Sergeant Man. Visit the principal Langdale Pikes before heading north to High Raise. Return along the winding spur of Gibson Knott and Helm Crag.

There are a variety of shorter routes making use of Stickle Ghyll, Dungeon Ghyll and Stake Pass, commencing from the head of Great Langdale.

Above:
The tips of the distant Langdale Pikes represented by the shapes of Harrison Stickle and Pavey Ark above the tower of the Church of St Mary, Rydal observed across the frosty parkland of Rydal Hall. The easily recognizable profiles of the Langdale Pikes occupy a place of affection in the hearts of most dedicated Lakeland walkers including myself. I think this is largely because they offer so much to so many. They present challenging climbing routes, the ultimate ways for safe scrambling and many other delights for more casual walkers and family groups. The youngsters of the latter can often be observed contentedly messing about around the shores of Stickle Tarn quite oblivious of the challenges awaiting their eventual attention above.

Right:
The purple heathers of Lingmoor Fell present a colourful foreground for this view of the Langdale Pikes. Left to right are the separate peaks of Pike of Stickle, Loft Crag, Thorn Crag, Harrison Stickle and some distance away Pavey Ark. One of the many alluring features of the Langdale Pikes is that within the space of an hour or so you can stand on several quite different craggy peaks, each with its own characteristics and views.

Left:

This photograph illustrates what I have already been preaching about, the almost infinite attractions to be discovered within the confines of the Langdale Pikes, from the tranquil, benign waters of Stickle Tarn to the challenging scramble up to the summit of Pavey Ark along the exposed grove of Jack's Rake. Both of these feature in this view. Jack's Rake must rank near to the ultimate sensible scramble for all those walkers who are not skilled in climbing techniques including the correct use of ropes. It is an exhilarating climb for those with a head for heights, but never venture up there after prolonged heavy rain. This is because the scar is a natural watercourse and I should not like you to experience, as I have, cascading water pouring down your back in its relentless search for the shortest and easiest path down!

Below left:

This shot is looking down on Stickle Tarn along the steep, rugged, relentless descent from Harrison Stickle. It was taken in December on a day of sunshine and showers and the contrasting light patterns changed by the minute. We had set out that particular day along Mickleden intent on climbing Scafell Pike and you can see that at the time this shot was taken, late in the afternoon, we were far away from reaching this intended objective. Honest, we were not lost! The explanation is that on reaching the top of Rossett Gill the weather towards The Scafells looked abominable whilst in contrast the Langdale Pikes were bathed in the most brilliant sunshine imaginable. The moral of this short story is that those who change their minds occasionally do not regret having done so!

Right:

A favourite spot for photographing the Langdale Pikes is from across the sheltered waters of Blea Tarn lying to the south, which is where this photograph was captured. The retreating winter snows also make a positive contribution to the fine views to be observed from around this tarn. I have spent many a pleasant hour at this spot, usually either early in the morning as a detour whilst motoring over to Eskdale or in the late evening observing the magnificent sunsets that are often visible from here. It is one of those spots that I never tire of returning to because the views from here of Side Pike and the Langdale Pikes will remain forever firm favourites of mine.

Above:
Taken from near the minor road linking Great Langdale with Little Langdale. The rising ground provides excellent views across the flat head of Great Langdale with its neatly arranged green pastures to the rugged, craggy, darker slopes of the Langdale Pikes of which the peak of Harrison Stickle is the highest.

On one occasion I came across a man working in an outdoor office up here equipped with all modern cons, including a computer! You don't believe me do you? Well inspect the proof of this assertion and let me hasten to vouch that there is no trick photography whatsoever involved.

10 Helvellyn Group

Location

North to south range of mountains dividing St John's in the Vale and Thirlmere to the West from Ullswater and Patterdale to the east.

Features

Long chain of interconnected, massive, dominant peaks. West slopes are generally rounded, the topmost ridges reasonably flat and the spectacular east faces a series of arêtes, intervening gouged-out combes some containing trapped tarns and sheer rock faces. The easterly slopes are the province of climbers and walkers experienced in exposed scrambling.

Principal peaks

Helvellyn : 3,118ft (950m) Lower Man : 3,033ft (925m) Nethermost Pike : 2,920ft (891m) Catstye Cam : 2,917ft (890m) Raise : 2,889ft (883m) Dollywaggon Pike : 2,810ft (858m) Great Dodd : 2,807ft (857m)

Favourite walking route

Climb Helvellyn from Wythburn. Scramble down Swirral Edge, walk round Red Tarn and climb back to the summit of Helvellyn along Striding Edge. Descend by way of Lower Man and Browncove Crags to Highpark Wood bordering Thirlmere. Use the forest trails to return to Wythburn. (Distance about 10 miles involving over 4,000ft of ascent: allow 7 hours.)

Other popular walking routes

A challenging linear route is from Threlkeld, south, along the Dodds and then over Raise to Helvellyn. This is followed by a descent by way of either Swirral Edge or Striding Edge into either Patterdale or Glenridding to rendezvous with your transport back.

Shorter but less exciting variants of the previ ously cited favourite route from Wythburn are: 1) to omit the arêtes encircling Red Tarn or 2) to descend southwards from the summit of Helvellyn to Grisedale Tarn and then to return to Wythburn by walking northwards up the forest trails.

Above:

A view of the summit of Helvellyn rising majestically above Grisedale. Also in the picture are the much trodden arête of Striding Edge and the pointed peak of Catstye Cam. A topping of autumn frost completes the composition. I have descended on many occasions into Patterdale along either Swirral Edge or Striding Edge eventually walking down the path clearly visible on the photograph. Strangely enough though, I have yet to climb on to Helvellyn from the Ullswater side. Perhaps there are many routes up and down high fells very familiar to you the joys of which you have yet to discover the other way round.

Right:

Walkers descending to Grisedale Tarn from Helvellyn . Beyond in partial shadow lies the massive ridge that links Fairfield to St Sunday Crag via Cofa Pike. This southerly route from Helvellyn travels over Nethermost and then Dollywaggon Pikes. This photograph is a particular favourite of mine because it happens to contain a fleeting glimpse of my wife, who at the time appeared to be more intent on overtaking the two gentlemen ahead of her than of waiting for me to catch up.

Below right:

A lingering cornice of pristine snow on the high slopes of Helvellyn competes for attention with the spectacular sharp-pointed ridge of Striding Edge climbing steeply from the east towards the crest of the mountain. Part of snaking Ullswater is visible within the uncompeting background. A little way below the spot from where this picture was taken there is a particularly revealing view of Striding Edge with part of Red Tarn appearing beyond. To get safely into this position is somewhat tricky and on this occasion the innocent but dangerous overhang of snow was sufficient to deter me from doing this until another day.

Left:

In my opinion one of the best panoramas from the summit area of Helvellyn is that down on to Red Tarn with the irregular shape of Ullswater leading the eyes away towards the distant Pennines. The walk right round the tarn is a very pleasant diversion, either by means of Swirral and Striding Edges or by keeping within a few feet of the edge of the water on the landward side! In my youth I once tried in vain to keep company with a fell runner round this circuit. We set off from Wythburn after breakfast, jogged the round and were back in Grasmere for a cool beer before lunch. I felt shattered after this escapade, whilst he was muttering something about going for a serious run that afternoon!

Right:

Looking down along Striding Edge out of the shadows near the summit of Helvellyn. There is normally such an intensity of two-way traffic along this extremely popular scramble that I heard that the next renovation programme might possibly include the installation of traffic lights! Walkers who trek along this arête at regular intervals are likely to experience extremes of weather conditions. The ridge is a very relaxing, easy scramble in still, clear weather but quite a different proposition in either strong, blustery winds or when covered in snow and ice. The most frightening occasion for me was when a sudden storm blew in accompanied by thunder and lightning and I was very relieved to get off the ridge without mishap.

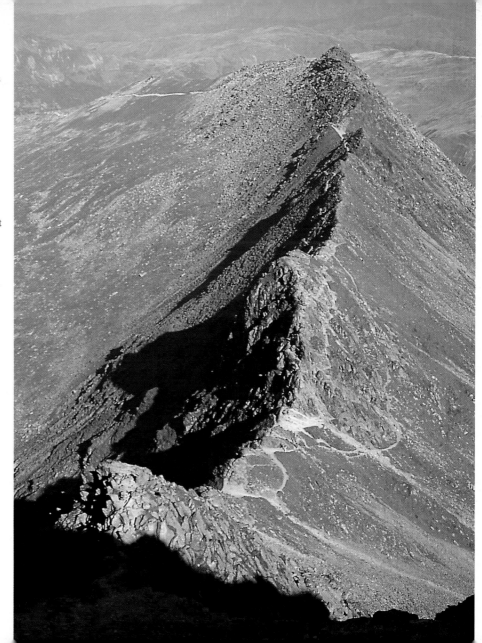

Above:

A long range view of the Dodds and of Helvellyn taken from the faraway slopes of Causey Pike. The shy summit of Helvellyn can just be made out together with the distinctive pointed cap of Catstye Cam. The north to south walk along the Dodds to Helvellyn can be either a misery or it can be exhilarating. On two occasions groups of us have battled along this exposed ridge during the height of summer in ferocious gales, wet through to our skins despite our light protective clothing and, moreover, frozen stiff in the process. The route was repeated shortly after these dismissive excursions on a hot, balmy, sunny day when a companion and I were reluctant to leave every single peak and I can assure you there are a lot of these about on this particular walk.

Left:

I was sitting in the cross shelter on Helvellyn on a bitterly cold day in April when two young and extremely cheerful climbers suddenly appeared over the sheer cliff face from the east, calmly stowed their crampons and ice axes away and invited me to join them for lunch. The photograph is of part of the extensive cooking equipment they happened to be carrying with them in order to do justice to their cordon bleu culinary skills.

11 The Fairfield Group

Location

An almost circular configuration of linked mountains. The westerly chain is a continuation southwards, beyond the fault-line of Grisedale, of the mighty Helvellyn Group. The easterly spur of the horseshoe separates the parallel valleys cut by Rydal Beck and Scandale Beck further to the east. At their southernmost tip the fells fall towards Ambleside.

Features

The group is dominated by the vast slopes of Fairfield, composed of gentle, rounded, grassy gradients on most faces but concealing treacherous steep, eroded combes and shattered rock pitches on its north to east flank. Some of the other major fells in this grouping, particularly Hart Crag and Dove Crag, possess similar features.

Principal peaks

Great Rigg : 2,513ft (766m) Fairfield : 2,863ft (873m) Hart Crag : 2,698ft (822m) Dove Crag : 2,603ft (792m)

Favourite walking route

Without doubt, the Fairfield Horseshoe. Starting from Ambleside either way round; clockwise the major peaks climbed are Heron Pike, Great Rigg, Fairfield, Hart Crag, Dove Crag and finally High and then Low Pikes. (Distance about 11 miles involving 3,100ft of ascent: allow 6 to 7 hours.)

Other popular walking routes

From Grasmere a variant of the Fairfield Horseshoe gaining the high ground of Heron Pike by way of Alcock Tarn. The return from Ambleside is by way of the low-level paths skirting either side of Rydal Water and Grasmere.

Climb Fairfield from Patterdale along St Sunday Crag and Cofa Pike. Descend westwards to Grisedale Tarn and from here walk northeastwards down Grisedale back into Patterdale.

Above:
A long distance view of snow-capped Fairfield and pointed Greatrigg Man from the bracken-laden slopes of Lingmoor Fell. The attractive village down below in Great Langdale valley is Chapel Stile. This view also shows the westerly flank of the great Fairfield Horseshoe. Starting from Rydal, cumulative height is gained by climbing up the steep slopes of Nab Scar, then on to Heron Pike, followed by an undulating trek to the helmet of Greatrigg Man and a final stroll up the gentle approach slopes leading to the vastness of Fairfield's summit area.

Left:
This photograph was taken during a descent of Wansfell Pike above Ambleside to reveal from a southeasterly viewpoint the complete Fairfield Horseshoe accentuated by areas of melting snow. In between is the narrow road that climbs tortuously over Kirkstone Pass. When walking the Horseshoe clockwise from Rydal the final descent is down the craggy peaks of, first, High and then Low Pikes. During the shortest days of winter always be careful to complete these rocky descents in daylight because some scrambling is involved and there are a variety of ways down which in the gathering dusk can be somewhat confusing.

Above right:
This exposure was taken with frozen fingers! These too were exposed on the climb to Greatrigg Man and the view is back, southwards, along the approach ridge from Heron Pike. The shimmering coastline can also be seen far away. Some distance further on that day we were engulfed in a swirling snow storm, the pelting, frozen flakes of which made visibility nigh impossible. A shadowy figure suddenly appeared out of the white void and in stumbling past he mumbled something like, 'You should have been up here yesterday when it was really bad!'

Right:
Looking east from just below the summit area of Fairfield . The valley is Deepdale and the massive, rocky slopes and intervening deep, dark, foreboding gullies are those that line the north edge of the flattish ribbon that links Fairfield to Hart Crag away to the east. Conditions that day were docile and we leisurely and carefully made our way right along this rim keeping to a narrow path of sorts no more than a few feet from a series of vertical voids. In more demanding weather conditions keep well to the south of this adventurous route and walk along the wide, well-worn main path that keeps to the flatter terrain.

Left:
Another one with a little snow on it. This was taken from the northeast corner of the Fairfield Horseshoe at a point where there are good continuous sightings of the major easterly fells. The more pointed peak centre-stage is The Knott and beyond this on the skyline the peaks of High Raise, Kidsty Pike and the shoulder of High Street can be identified. Most of us probably enjoy the thrill of walking through soft, dry, pristine, powder snow; I know I do. Although we experience relatively mild winters, on many occasions the top 500ft or so of the highest fells in Lakeland get annual doses of the stuff. Should a spell of cold, frosty, sunny weather follow any such fall, the crystalline flakes are likely to remain for quite a spell and of all conditions these, in my opinion, are the very best to be amongst in exploring the high fells.

Below left:
The long shadows of trees in winter cast from the low orbit of the rising sun on the frozen, frosty parkland at Rydal Hall. High above are the snow-covered peaks of the Fairfield Horseshoe which challenge you to test your skills and determination on their steep, slippery slopes. To walk the horseshoe in such conditions is great but I will let you experience this for yourself. Sometimes it can be different! Once I was with a party when we encountered incessant, heavy rain the whole way round. I soon abandoned taking notes, somewhat carelessly stuffing my notebook away in the only partly closed pocket of my storm-proof anorak. Needless to say, I spent several days after this trying to decipher notes I had taken previously, by toasting the notebook over an open fire page by page.

12 High Street and the Easterly Fells

Location

The several long, north to south running ridges situated to the east of Ullswater and Patterdale, Kirkstone and Troutbeck. They occupy a vast area and their most easterly slopes descend to Haweswater Reservoir and Kentmere.

Features

Long, rounded, for the most part grassy ridges with interconnecting rocky spurs. These are punctuated by delightful sheltered valleys some of which support hill farms. Several impressively large high-level tarns are scattered within this area including Angle Tarn, Hayeswater, Blea Water, and Kentmere Reservoir.

Principal peaks

High Street : 2,718ft (828m) High Raise : 2,634ft (802m) Thornthwaite Crag : 2,569ft (784m) Harter Fell : 2,539ft (778m) Ill Bell : 2,476ft (757m)

Favourite walking route

Starting from Hartsop climb The Knott by way of Hayeswater. Then on to High Street and Thornthwaite Crag. Return along the ridge terminating in Gray Crag. (Distance about 7 miles involving 2,300ft of ascent: allow 4 to 5 hours.)

Other popular walking routes

Kentmere Horseshoe. From Kentmere walk round Kentmere Pike, Harter Fell, Mardale Ill Bell, Thornthwaite Crag, Froswick, Ill Bell and Yoke.

There are many delightful walks starting from Patterdale that explore the fells and valleys extending east towards Haweswater Reservoir. These encompass Place Fell, Rest Dodd, High Raise, Red Crag and the remote valleys of Boredale and Martindale.

Above:

A revealing view of the folded easterly fells dominated by the bulk of High Street taken from the easterly rim of the Fairfield Horseshoe. The easterly fells, as can be seen from this photograph, offer many fine ridge routes for walkers. Most of the eastern fells, with the exception of some of those forming the Kentmere Horseshoe, lie within the radius of a comfortable day's walking from the tiny and delightful hamlet of Hartsop. Fortunately there are usually adequate cheap car parking facilities in this area, either at the far end of the village or at Low Wood near Brothers Water.

Left:
The tranquil waters of Angle Tarn. Which one? — the one in the easterly fells of course! This refreshing stretch of water is situated in a shallow basin beneath the protection of Angletarn Pikes, Heck Crag, Buck Crag, Satura Crag, Brock Crags and Lingy Crag. What a lot of lofty guardians! Although I have passed this way on several occasions I have never found time to linger there, but I have vowed that the next time I am in this vicinity I will do just this.

Right:
The rocky heights leading to Gray Crag provide many safe viewing platforms for looking down on Hayeswater Reservoir tucked away in the narrow valley to the east cut by Hayeswater Gill. Gray Crag provides a super ridge walk either up to or down from Thornthwaite Crag. I was along here on one occasion battling up in the teeth of a ferocious gale, trying desperately to hold my woollen hat on with the aid of both hands, when some other walkers appeared descending the rocky slope. One of these cheerfully commented, 'Be careful it's a wee bit breezy up there!'

Left:

There cannot be a taller cairn anywhere in Lakeland than the splendid beacon marking the summit of Thornthwaite Crag, unless of course you happen to know otherwise. The surrounding rocks are a mecca for walkers to stop at, to eat some refreshments there, pass the time of day with fellow addicts and to admire the views southwards towards Ill Bell and far-off Windermere. However, beware of the ferocious sheep that wander around this spot! They are so tame and used to being fed by generous walkers that over the years they have mutated into a most aggressive strain who will devour almost anything, including having a go at you if you give them half a chance.

Below left:

This revealing view was taken just below the summit of High Street, slightly to the northeast of it. The long, spur leading down to Haweswater Reservoir is Riggindale Crag and the valley to the left and north of this is not surprisingly that of Riggindale. The rounded, northern approach slopes leading to High Street around here are named Racecourse Hill which probably gives some passing amusement to walkers who quite often will be able to observe shaggy hill ponies grazing contentedly on these grasslands and who I do not believe would muster a gallop even if you held out strawberries to them.

Right:

Taken on the descent from High Street towards Ill Bell which is the prominent, pointed peak captured in the centre of the photograph. Part of Windermere can also be seen snaking away in the far distance many hundreds of feet below and several miles away. Ill Bell is a great mountain and one of the rewards for reaching its interesting summit is that you have a choice of no less than three competing symmetrical cairns to lean your weary limbs against. The fell is part of the Kentmere Horseshoe on which I have enjoyed many escapades, such as the one illustrated by the final photograph in this section.

Right:

Well these long, high mountain ridges were used by the Romans as mainline communication routes! These apprentice gladiators were practising their skills on the slopes of Harter Fell. They were both useless and I had little hesitation in turning both my thumbs down. Fortunately for them I could not find any lions at the time.

13 The Coniston Fells

Location

Situated to the northwest of Coniston Water and lying between the Duddon valley further west and Wrynose Pass and Little Langdale to the north.

Features

A discrete grouping of high, barren fells linked together by bands of rock. The easterly slopes of Coniston Old Man have suffered the ravages of extensive mining operations but elsewhere this superb mountainous terrain has been expertly carved by the hand of nature alone to produce a mixture of rounded slopes, rock scattered cols and some superb climbing pitches, particularly on Dow Crag.

Principal peaks

Coniston Old Man : 2,635ft (803m) Swirl How : 2,630ft (802m) Dow Crag : 2,555ft (779m) Wetherlam : 2,502ft (762m)

Favourite walking route

From Coniston head west along the Walna Scar Road. Then up the ridge leading to Dow Crag en route to Coniston Old Man. The circuitous return is via Swirl How and Wetherlam by way of Prison Band. (Distance about 11 miles involving 3,750ft of ascent: allow 7 to 8 hours.)

Other popular walking routes

Climb the Old Man directly from Coniston. Then walk north along the band to Swirl How. Descend into Greenburn by means of Wet Side Edge and return via Tilberthwaite and Hole Rake Pass.

On either of the above routes a slight diversion from Swirl How to the summit of Grey Friar is very rewarding for the commanding views it affords west and northwestwards across the intervening valleys of the Duddon and Mosedale towards the Scafells.

Above:

The southern, distant profiles of the Coniston Fells observed across Torver Back Common above Coniston Water. One of many small tarns situated in these folded, lower fells make a fine, contrasting foreground for the higher mountains. The two most prominent groupings on this photograph are the long, craggy ridge in the centre leading to the heights of Dow Crag and the vast, more-rounded slopes to the east (right) which rise to Coniston Old Man. You can stand on the tops of each of these mountains comfortably within the space of an hour or so.

Right:

Taken from the summit of Coniston Old Man of two-way traffic progressing in heavy lying snow along the band leading northwards to Swirl How. The Scafells and their satellite high peaks provide the inevitable wintry back-cloth. The walk that day had been an impromptu affair. The decision to go had been taken after the late night weather forecast only some few hours earlier, a quick dash up the motorway from Cheshire at some unearthly hour that morning, boots on in the Coniston car park by 9am, on top of the Old Man by way of Dow Crag towards lunchtime, a quick visit to Swirl How in the afternoon, an adventurous descent along Prison Band and back home in Cheshire for a late supper. But what a day, 13 January 1991; you may have had the good fortune to have been there too!

Below right:

The wooded lushness of Great Langdale valley around Elter Water is captured in this shot taken from the bracken-clad slopes of Loughrigg Fell. High above lies the sprawling bulk of mighty Wetherlam and the long ridge of Wet Side Edge leading majestically down from the heights of Swirl How over Great and Little Carrs. All routes I have tried down from Wetherlam and Swirl How into Little Langdale have had their frustrations. Based on these experiences may I proffer two pieces of advice. When descending along Wetherlam Edge veer left off the main spur about half way down as the gradient temporarily flattens out at a spot marked by an insignificant cairn. Towards the end of the descent by way of Wet Side Edge veer right well before you somewhat surprisingly reach private land, and cross Greenburn Beck above the stretch where it gushes through a steepish fall of rocks.

Left:

The clear, still, copper sulphate blue liquid of Low Water affords a welcome respite when climbing directly up Coniston Old Man from the village along the steep slopes that contain seemingly endless quarry spoils. Most walkers linger here for a spell but perhaps not for too long on days like the one on which this photograph was taken. The walker is me taking a momentary pause, but I have also languished at this spot on blazing hot days. One of these immediately comes to mind when three of us bathed in the tarn sporting only handkerchiefs, bits of string and a Boys' Brigade belt with which we happened to be prepared.

Below left:

I believe the views on and around the summit of Wetherlam are some of the finest in the whole of Lakeland. This one was taken on a peach of a day in October and is from just below the summit, my camera pointing across Little Langdale towards Helvellyn and Fairfield. I believe I deserved to get this rewarding picture because the previous day our fickle weather had tantalised me into climbing up Wetherlam twice and each time I got within camera distance of my summit objective, heavy curtains of mountain cloud were unceremoniously brought together to thwart my peeping into the valleys far below.

Appendix: Principal fells indicating their groupings (1)

Fell	Height (Per OS Maps etc.) Feet	Metres	1	2	3	4	5	6	7	8	9	10	11	12	13
Fells over 3,000 feet															
1 Scafell Pike	3,210	978							*						
2 Scafell	3,162	964							*						
3 Helvellyn	3,118	950										*			
4 Broad Crag	3,100	945							*						
5 Ill Crag	3,070	935							*						
6 Skiddaw	3,053	931	*												
7 Lower Man (Helvellyn)	3,033	925										*			
Fells between 2,501 and 3,000 feet															
8 Great End	2,984	910							*						
9 Bow Fell	2,960	902								*					
10 Great Gable	2,949	899						*							
11 Pillar	2,927	892					*								
12 Nethermost Pike	2920	891										*			
13 Catstye Cam	2,917	890										*			
14 Esk Pike	2,903	885								*					
15 Raise	2,889	883										*			
16 Fairfield	2,863	873											*		
17 Blencathra (Saddleback)	2,847	868	*												
18 Little Man (Skiddaw)	2,837	865	*												
19 White Side	2832	863										*			
20 Crinkle Crags	2,816	859								*					
21 Dollywaggon Pike	2,810	858										*			
22 Great Dodd	2,807	857										*			
23 Grasmoor	2,791	852		*											
24 Stybarrow Dodd	2,770	843										*			
25 Scoat Fell	2,760	841					*								
26 St Sunday Crag	2,756	841											*		
27 Crag Hill	2,749	839		*											
28 High Street	2,718	828												*	
29 Red Pike (Mosedale)	2,707	826					*								
30 Hart Crag	2,698	822											*		
31 Steeple	2,687	819					*								
32 Lingmell	2,649	807							*						
33 High Stile	2,644	806				*									
34 Coniston Old Man	2,635	803													*
35 High Raise (Haweswater)	2,634	802												*	
36 Kirk Fell	2,630	802						*							
37 Swirl How (Coniston Fells)	2,630	802													*
38 Green Gable	2,628	801						*							
39 Haycock	2,618	797					*								
40 Brim Fell	2,611	796													*

Principal fells indicating their groupings (2)

	Fell	Height (Per OS Maps etc.)		Mountain Grouping												
		Feet	Metres	1	2	3	4	5	6	7	8	9	10	11	12	13
41	Dove Crag	2,603	792											*		
42	Grisedale Pike	2,593	791		*											
43	Watson Dodd	2,584	789										*			
44	Rampsgill Head	2,581	792		*											
45	Great Carrs	2,575	785													*
46	Allen Crags	2,572	785						*							
47	Thornthwaite Crag	2,569	784												*	
48	Glaramara	2,560	781						*							
49	Kidsty Pike	2,560	780												*	
50	Dow Crag	2,555	779													*
51	Red Screes	2,541	776												*	
52	Harter Fell (Mardale)	2,539	778												*	
53	Grey Friar	2,536	773													*
54	Wandope	2,533	772		*											
55	Sail	2,530	773		*											
56	Hopegill Head	2,525	770		*											
57	Great Rigg	2,513	766											*		
58	Stony Cove Pike	2,502	763												*	
59	Wetherlam	2,502	762													*

Selected fells between 2,001 and 2,500 feet

	Fell	Feet	Metres	1	2	3	4	5	6	7	8	9	10	11	12	13
60	High Raise	2,500	762									*				
61	Slight Side	2,499	760							*						
62	Ill Bell (Mardale)	2,496	761												*	
63	Red Pike (Buttermere)	2,479	755				*									
64	Ill Bell	2,476	757												*	
65	Dale Head	2,473	753			*										
66	Carl Side	2,448	746	*												
67	High Crag (Buttermere)	2,443	744				*									
68	The Knott	2,423	739												*	
69	Robinson	2,417	737			*										
70	Sergeant Man	2,414	736									*				
71	Harrison Stickle	2,403	732									*				
72	Kentmere Pike	2,397	730												*	
73	Hindscarth	2,385	727			*										
74	Froswick	2,359	719												*	
75	Pike of Stickle	2,323	708									*				
76	Whiteside	2,317	706		*											
77	Yoke	2,309	704												*	
78	Pike of Blisco	2,304	705								*					
79	Pavey Ark	2,288	697									*				
80	Gray Crag	2,286	697												*	

Note: The above imperial and metric measurements of height have been extracted from the relevant Ordnance Survey maps. There are some minor anomolies between these two sets of measurements that are not explained by rounding off differences.